I can
change
the world

Queen
I will wear my hair like a crown!

I am a good friend.

What I have to say, matters

I can shine like the brightest stars!

I am glad I am ME!

I'm bold, beautiful, and brilliant

I can do difficult things
FINISH FINISH FINIS
INISH FINISH
5234
FINIS NISH FINISH NISH FINIS

So many colors
is what makes
a rainbow beautiful.

I'm a helper
I'm a helper

I am a girl who has a lot of ideas

I can be anything I set my mind to

I am unique and important

The sky is the limit for me!
State University

I'M UNSTOPPABLE
U

I will dance
to my own beat!
GROOVE

I get back up when I fall

My heart
is full of
KINDNESS and COURAGE

I will let myself sparkle
Funky

My smile brightens the room!

I am brave enough to try.

Learning is my superpower

I'm enough

www.ingramcontent.com/pod-product-compliance
Lightning Source LLC
Chambersburg PA
CBHW081024040426
42444CB00014B/3336
9781945056994